Copyleft 2024. No rights reserved.

ISBN-13:
978-1-7374438-6-5

All photos taken by Anne Mitchell and Chuck Shuman. Written by Anne Mitchell. Designed by Suzanne King.

We CAN Plant...

NATIVE PLANTS

for ecosystems and habitats

by Anne Mitchell and Suzanne King

TABLE OF CONTENTS

ENDORSMENTS + REVIEWS
- JONAH PFLUG 6
- MARIE BECKER 7
- LOGAN WADDLE 8
- STEPHANIE + RICHARD BENNETT 9

OPENING QUOTE
- STEFANO MANCUSO 10

THE STORY
- COMING FROM GRATITUDE
  — MILLIE 12
- HONORING OUR PAIN FOR THE WORLD
  — LEARNING ABOUT LAWNS 16
- SEEING WITH NEW EYES
  — EVERYTHING CHANGED 18
- GOING FORTH
  — MORE POWER THAN WE THINK WE HAVE ... 22

THE TECHNIQUE + *before and after* 30

RESOURCES and CONCLUSION 34

ABOUT THE AUTHOR-GARDENER 36

plus A NOTE ABOUT THE STORY

THE GENERAL STRUCTURE OF THE STORY IS INSPIRED BY JOANNA MACY'S SPIRAL FROM THE WORK THAT RECONNECTS

> COMING FROM GRATITUDE
> HONORING OUR PAIN FOR THE WORLD
> SEEING WITH NEW EYES
> GOING FORTH

THE STORY DOESN'T INCLUDE THE SPIRAL EXPLICITLY BUT WE'RE INCLUDING IT HERE TO PAY RESPECT TO ITS ROLE IN OUR THINKING, AND TO POINT ANYONE WHO'S INTERESTED TO THE WORK THAT RECONNECTS.

→ WORKTHATRECONNECTS.ORG

PRAISE for

We CAN Plant...

> "This book is the perfect introduction into transforming your yard and provides great resources for taking that next step to support biodiversity."
>
> —Jonah Pflug, Aerospace Engineer

"Anne's dedication to the natural world can be clearly seen in the vibrant ecosystem she has welcomed into her backyard.

In *We Can Plant...*, Anne tells a compelling story about the interconnection of gardening and climate resiliency. She introduces us to ecologically-minded gardening, why it's important, and how to get started. Along the way, we meet bullfrogs, butterflies, and a stunning array of native plants.

We have the power — and onus — to invest in our spaces for the greater good. It doesn't matter if you have a 10' x 12' yard or 6 acres, you can make a difference in your local ecosystem and this book will help you get started."

— Marie Becker,
Native Garden Designer
@ Spotts Garden Center

More Praise for We Can Plant...

> "Anne and Suzanne have done a tremendous job outlining the ecological, environmental, and financial benefits of native landscapes in urban settings in this publication.
>
> Their commitment to implementing and managing native plant, insect, and animal-friendly habitat is both commendable and inspirational despite constant climate adversity. Their book serves as both a case study and roadmap for landowners of any type to implement native, biodiversity-friendly landscaping practices in their own respective setting.
>
> I'd recommend this guide to anyone willing to learn about the benefits of environmentally conscious gardening and the importance of implementing these efforts in their own landscape."

—Logan Waddle,
Sustainability Program Leader

> Small acts are the drivers of life and of the human experience on this planet. While we are constantly bombarded with news, media, and stories of large acts like elections, medical breakthroughs, multi-million dollar engineering projects or movie releases, I believe it remains the small acts of everyday people that are the most consequential and important.
>
> This book is one of those small acts.
>
> This book is a gift to its readers of experience and hard-won knowledge. I have known Anne Mitchell for several years now, and it is through her daily small acts of gardening, cooking, reading, learning, and connecting with folks all over the country that she is impacting lives and experiences on this planet.
>
> I urge you, reader, to find inspiration and fellowship in this book and in the experiences that Anne shares within these pages. Your small acts too will make a difference for you and those around you.

— Stephanie + Richard Bennett

"It is my impression that most people don't really understand how important plants are for human existence.

Of course, everyone knows - or at least I hope they do - that we are able to breathe because of the oxygen produced by plants, and the entire food chain, and thus the food that nourishes all animals on Earth, relies on plants.

But how many people realize that oil, coal, gas, and all the so-called non-renewable energy sources are nothing more than another form of energy that was trapped by plants millions of years ago?

Or that the most active ingredients in many of our most important medicines come from plants?

Or that wood, with all its amazing characteristics, is still the most widely used building material in much of the world?

Our lives, as well as the lives of every other animal on this planet, depend upon the plant world. "

— Stefano Mancuso, *The Evolutionary Genius of Plants*

I'D LIKE TO INTRODUCE YOU TO Millie.

SHE'S THE CHRISTMAS CACTUS IN THE FOREGROUND; THE DOG SITTING NEAR HER IS NIKI.

CHRISTMAS CACTUS
SCHLUMBERGERA

BASENJI
CANINE

MILLIE IS THE DAUGHTER OF MY GRANDMOTHER'S CHRISTMAS CACTUS. MY GRANDMOTHER DIED IN 1973 AND MY MOTHER TOOK CUTTINGS FROM THAT PLANT FOR HERSELF AND EACH OF HER CHILDREN.

This plant has been with me ever since — she went to college with me, and we've moved all over the country. She instilled in me a love of life and a connection with the more-than-human world.

She led me to garden in every home I've ever lived in. She spends summers outside on our screened porch now but at other houses she spent the summer on a deck and once hosted a family of wrens who chose to build their house in her pot, under her leaves.

She still lives with me and she blooms every year — sometimes extravagantly, sometimes quite modestly, but she always blooms.

Most of my gardening was for my own aesthetic benefit — those plants I found beautiful and that brought a smile or a sense of satisfaction to me. I used the design that reflected the human cultural norms of the places I lived.

Notice the very neat plant spacing and mulch and mostly non-native plants.

I DIDN'T KNOW ANY BETTER.

Over time, I've begun to more fully understand the devastation humans have delivered to the more-than-human world — changing most of the natural world to suit our needs, our sense of beauty and order. Estimates are that humans have had a substantial impact on 95% of all land on Earth. It's astonishing to contemplate.

And most of what we've done is negative. We have devasted ecosystems, displacing ecologically important plants and the animals who rely on them, fundamentally changing ecosystems — and our entire climate — worldwide.

In less than 100 years, we've reduced our yards to contaminated expanses of non-native turf grass that doesn't support any life and destroys our soil, air, and water quality, requires extensive maintenance, chemical inputs and loads of water — yet we call it "pristine" and "well-managed" and "beautiful". Turf grass lawns were not the norm in the U.S.A. before WWII. They're really quite new, brought over from Europe, not an "age-old tradition".

NANCY LAWSON SAYS:

"One of the many tragedies of the common era is that the spaces we live, work and play have been shoehorned into conformity, designed to be uniform and boring and flat for the sake of convenience and profit. What a great loss to us as participants in this world – in every sense: aesthetically, tactily, aurally, olfactorily and gustatorily. And what an even greater loss to all the other creatures who could thrive in more varied landscapes."

(find Nancy's work @ HUMANEGARDENER.COM)

OBEDIENT PLANT
PHYSOTEGIA VIRGINIANA

When I began understanding the value of gardening with native plants (meaning plants that evolved over millenia in this place with all other life forms here) and the power of those plants to restore biodiversity, everything changed.

Native plants are absolutely gorgeous. There are so many more than I ever knew about. And many are quite unique.

These plants and all the more-than-human beings here have evolved to rely on each other for housing, food, security and play. They need each other and we need all of them. Everyone has a role to play and we cannot survive without each other. After bringing native plants into the yard, the bees and butterflies and moths have returned in large numbers. There are many more birds — both those who live here all year and migrants, flying through on their way to summer or winter homes.

HARDY HIBISCUS
ROSE MALLOW
HIBISCUS LAEVIS

SAW-TOOTH SUNFLOWER
HELIANTHUS GROSSESERRATUS

MEADOW BLAZING STAR
LIATRIS LIGULISTYLUS

BULLFROGS MOVED TO OUR POND AFTER I BROUGHT NATIVE PLANTS INTO THE YARD BUT THEY DIDN'T SHOW UP FOR THE NINE YEARS THE POND WAS HERE WITHOUT NATIVE PLANTS.

COINCIDENCE? I DON'T THINK SO.

THE HAWK IS A FREQUENT VISITOR AND THOUGH I'M OFTEN SADDENED WHEN HE FINDS DINNER, I ALSO BELIEVE A TRUE ECOSYSTEM IS FUNCTIONING HERE.

THERE'S STILL A LOT WE DON'T KNOW OR ARE JUST FIGURING OUT.

ACCORDING TO NANCY LAWSON:

"ONLY RECENTLY HAVE RESEARCHERS BEGUN TO UNDERSTAND THE SOCIAL AND SCENT BASED DYNAMICS OF CREATURES LIKE SNAKES, DISCOVERING THAT THEY TOO COMMUNE WITH FRIENDS, DEFEND YOUNG, AND BABYSIT FOR ONE ANOTHER. A LOT OF THE REASON THAT WE DIDN'T DEEM THEM CAPABLE OF ALL THESE THINGS IS THAT WE CAN'T EXPERIENCE IT: THEY ARE COMMUNICATING IN WAYS WE DON'T."

I'VE SEEN SNAKES AROUND OUR POND BUT THEY WON'T SIT STILL LONG ENOUGH FOR ME TO GET A PHOTO.

I NOW GARDEN IN SUPPORT OF *life,*
NOT ONLY FOR MY OWN AESTHETICS.

YELLOW POND LILY
NUPHAR LUTEA

AMERICAN WATER WILLOW
JUSTICIA AMERICANA

MY UNDERSTANDING OF WHAT IS "*pretty*" OR "*appropriate*" OR "*neat*" HAS CHANGED DRAMATICALLY.

NATURE IS FULL, ABUNDANT, BURSTING WITH COLOR AND TEXTURE.

OHIO SPIDERWORT
TRADESCANTIA OHIENSIS

EACH PLANT PROVIDES SOMETHING FOR SOMEONE ELSE.

I believe we are facing enormous challenges in the coming decades and life can feel overwhelming.

I know many of us are worried and sad.

Biodiversity loss, climate change, air and water quality, health concerns, inequalities, political upheaval and more — all of it is stressful and often feels bigger than us, more than we can handle.

However,
we have way more power than we think we have. We have love. We can have a meaningful impact on supporting biodiversity just based on the plants we choose to bring into our yards and how we care for them.

I LIVE ON A 75 FOOT WIDE BY 150 FOOT LONG LOT IN A *very* INDUSTRIALIZED AREA AND THERE IS A HOUSE AND GARAGE ON THAT LOT.

AMERICAN WATER WILLOW
JUSTICIA AMERICANA

YELLOW POND LILY
NUPHAR LUTEA

THERE IS NO TURF GRASS ANYMORE. AND LIFE IS THRIVING ON THAT LAND.

I STOPPED USING HERBICIDES, FERTILIZERS AND PESTICIDES A COUPLE OF DECADES AGO AND I'M NOT OVERRUN WITH PROBLEM INSECTS OR PLANTS - THOUGH IT IS DIFFICULT TO KEEP ALL THE INVASIVE PLANTS OUT OF THE SPACE. I BELIEVE THAT WILL BECOME EASIER AS MORE NATIVE PLANTS GROW TO MATURITY.

WHEEL BUG NYMPH A.K.A. ASSASSIN BUG NYMPH

BROWN PAPER WASP EATING A LARVA

FOR EXAMPLE, WHEN APHIDS SHOW UP, I SIMPLY WATCH AND WITHIN A WEEK OR TWO OTHER INSECTS HAVE TAKEN CARE OF THEM AND I HAVE DONE NOTHING.

TALL IRONWEED
VERNONIA GIGANTEA

Sometimes a plant or a group of plants will be eaten entirely by animals, often rabbits or squirrels. And while I'm frustrated by losing the money I spent on the plants and the time I spent planting and caring for them, I know the rabbits don't have a grocery store where they can buy their food. I do. And I am complicit in taking away their resources. So I don't worry much about it and I plant more in the hopes of supporting more animals.

It's fascinating and fun to watch the native plants rearrange themselves as they find the conditions that suit them best.

Some of those plants have grown much larger than expected, probably from the years I brought in compost and mulch to support the non-native plants I used to have.

GOLDENROD
SOLIDAGO

Native plants don't need anything more than what is already there — they fix the soil without much help from humans. They have very deep root systems allowing them to find buried nutrients and handle different rain patterns and fluctuations in temperatures. They're adapted to our soil type. They've evolved to provide food and shelter to native insects, birds, and other animals. And they're beautiful on top of all that. It's really mystical and miraculous.

WILD QUININE
PARTHENIUM INTEGRIFOLIUM

I've also found that some native plants don't like my garden and won't stay. Others just show up — almost as if their friends called them and asked them to move in. I can't explain it all, but I can enjoy it.

Every month changes so the garden is always new. Yes, there are often holes in the leaves or missing leaves but there are also butterfly caterpillars and lots of songbirds.

There is less work as I learn to leave the garden alone - allowing leaves to decompose on the ground providing mulch and then compost for the new plants; leaving fallen limbs in a stack on the ground to provide housing for insects and safe spaces for birds and small mammals during storms; keeping plants upright in winter so that both migrant and local birds can continue eating the seeds and insects can nest in hollow stems; not "cleaning up" in spring - all of this is beautiful and supports many more-than-humans who share this space with us. Even snow is prettier on plants than on lawn.

Browns and golds are colors too - and are beautiful.

AND THE GARDEN SUPPORTS LIFE EVEN IN THE COLDEST MONTHS. ONE ROBIN CLAIMED OUR AMERICAN BEAUTY BUSHES FOR HIMSELF THIS YEAR AND ATE THE BERRIES ALL WINTER LONG AND RAN OFF ANYONE ELSE WHO TRIED TO GET NEAR THOSE BUSHES.

HE ALSO YELLED AT ME WHEN I GOT TOO CLOSE SO WE ACTUALLY ESTABLISHED SOME SORT OF RELATIONSHIP AND NOW THAT HE'S MOVED ON, I MISS HIM.

AMERICAN BEAUTYBERRY

CALICARPA AMERICANA

NATURE, AND ALL THE MORE-THAN-HUMAN BEINGS, ARE MUCH SMARTER THAN WE TEND TO BELIEVE. WE JUST NEED TO CATCH UP.

AND AS MAYA ANGELOU SAID:
"DO THE BEST YOU CAN WITH WHAT YOU KNOW. AND WHEN YOU KNOW BETTER, DO BETTER."

I KNOW BETTER NOW.

HOW TO GET RID OF YOUR LAWN
with *lasagna gardening*

BEFORE

AFTER/NOW

HOW TO GET RID OF YOUR LAWN
with *lasagna gardening*

① START IN EARLY SPRING OR SEPTEMBER — "LASAGNA" SHEET MULCHING NEEDS TO "COOK" FOR ABOUT 6 MONTHS BEFORE PLANTING. MAKE SURE YOUR GRASS IS MOWED VERY LOW.

② GATHER CARDBOARD*♥ AND START COVERING.

* SUGGESTIONS: APPLIANCE STORE, MATTRESS STORE, OR BIKE SHOP
♥ NO GLOSSY CARDBOARD. REMOVE ALL TAPE.

③ COVER ALL THE GRASS YOU'RE GETTING RID OF — NO GAPS!

④ WATER THE CARDBOARD.

WATERING HELPS BREAK DOWN THE CARDBOARD AND SENDS THE SIGNAL TO WORMS & MICROBES TO MOVE IN

⑤ ADD YOUR WATER FEATURE (IF WANTED).

⑥ ADD 3" OF COMPOST⁺ᵛ AND 2" OF MULCH.▲

+ DECOMPOSING LEAVES MAKE GOOD COMPOST

ᵛ LESS NECESSARY FOR NATIVE PLANTS SINCE THEY'RE ALREADY ADAPTED TO OUR SOIL TYPES

▲ DON'T SKIP THIS STEP

⑦ AFTER LETTING IT ALL SIT FOR 6 MONTHS, START PLACING AND PLANTING PLANTS.

⑧ ENJOY THE PROCESS AND BEAUTY OF GARDENING FOR LIFE.

SOME FINAL WORDS

We are offering this book as an introduction to one method of converting lawn to habitat. We're focusing on our own experiences, over a period of time, in one urban residential lot, to show the power and impact of growing native plants.

While most people won't choose to completely eradicate their lawns and replace them with native plants, we do hope to inspire people to consider converting a part of their lawns to native plants — and to consider the fun of watching many beings return to our yards and the joy we can feel in supporting life and mitigating biodiversity loss.

With deep gratitude for your interest in native plants and for considering your role in restoring biodiversity,

Anne + Suzanne

and DEDICATIONS

We dedicate this book to all the people who have inspired us, supported us, and offered insights into our gardening and the evolution of this little book: our partners, Chuck & Benjamin; all who reviewed our work; members of the Speedway Gardening Club; the skillful gardeners at Spotts Garden Center; friends and family who have watched the development of this one garden and played with their own gardening practices. Each and every one of you are involved in this project and we appreciate you all.

AND RESOURCES

There are many methods to consider in making this change. We're focusing on only one - known as lasagna gardening or sheet mulching. There are other methods and there are many resources that can help with making the decision and the specific strategy to use.

Homegrown National Park and Wild Ones are both non-profits that offer a phenomenal range of very specific tools to support us in figuring out how to do this — as well as ethical considerations and a community of others working towards the same goals.

Wild Ones connects people & native plants with a growing number of U.S. chapters.

→ WILDONES.ORG

Homegrown National Park® (HNP) works to add native plants and remove invasive ones where we live, work, learn, pray, and play.

→ HOMEGROWNNATIONALPARK.ORG

Additionally, nearly every U.S. state and Canadian province has a native plant society, so you can likely find localized support too.

For a list, check out the North American Native Plant Society at:

→ NANPS.ORG/NATIVE-PLANT-SOCIETIES

About the Author - Gardener
Anne Mitchell

I found in native plant gardening what I had not found previously - purpose, connection, and joy. I grew up wanting to change the world, make it a better place, a sentiment I think many people share, though we don't often talk about. I got a degree in social work and began working with people labeled as cognitively different and found ways - with lots of other people as all good work is done in the company of others - to bring labeled people into community life.

It was good work and I learned a lot, but the system has a way of distorting good work back into business as usual, and I found myself dissatisfied with the outcomes, fighting more than creating. I moved to learning more about community building and found some satisfaction in asset based community development work. And yet, there too, the system posed so many barriers and I found myself protesting, fighting rather than creating and collaborating. And as time continued, the global crises we face - climate change, biodiversity loss, inequality in so many ways and on so many levels - have grown real and urgent to me and I began to lose hope.

I have always loved plants and gardening though I focused on creating a yard full of beautiful exotic flowers with some veggies for good measure. That was good work too but a lot of hard work that required lots of inputs - compost, water, new plants, weeding. I stumbled onto native plants when nothing would grow under my front yard sugar maple tree until I discovered Carex, a sedge native to North America. Magical things seemed to happen when the Carex not only grew under the maple tree but allowed other plants to grow as well.

I began planting more Carex into my back yard sunny garden and discovered more and more about the wisdom of native plants and their role in supporting life. In the years since, I have converted most of my yard to native plants and magical things continue to happen - the plants thrive, bringing beauty, but they also feed the insects and birds and small mammals. And my work has decreased as I trust the plants and animals to do theirs. I am constantly amazed at the life that shares this little plot of land with me.

I have come to believe that my contribution has to do with more fully understanding my role and responsibility to all of life, not just to myself or even just to other humans. I make a lot of mistakes but nature is quite forgiving and resilient. We depend on our ecosystem to support us and we can support her too. I hope to share some of what I've learned and to learn a lot more.

We can turn this around and we can do so starting in our own backyards. It's not more complicated than that. I now feel a sense of connection that I haven't felt in a long time — I belong and so do the blue-winged wasps, the black swallowtail butterflies, the yellow rumped warblers and eastern bluebirds, the rabbits and possum and all the other life carrying on their tasks here each day. And in that connection are moments of joy I hope everyone experiences now and then.

As I write this I am watching the rain fall on the golden amsonia foliage, the goldenrod, aster and perennial sunflower stalks drop their seeds, while some late blooming rudbeckia still stand proudly.

Purpose, connection and joy — that is great work.

You can find more of my work at Game B Press — gamebpress.com

www.ingramcontent.com/pod-product-compliance
Lightning Source LLC
Chambersburg PA
CBHW041522070526
44585CB00002B/44